WHY I
SHOUT

31 REASONS

★ TO REJOICE ★

IN
THE
LORD

FOREWORD BY **THOMAS WESLEY WEEKS, SR.**
A MONTH OF MEDITATIONS FOR YOUR DAILY JOURNEY TO FREEDOM

WHY I
SHOUT

31 REASONS

★ TO REJOICE ★

IN THE LORD

BY **SHARON NZWALLA RYAN**
WITH **CHRISTOPHER CAPEN RYAN**

XULON PRESS

Xulon Press
2301 Lucien Way #415
Maitland, FL 32751
407.339.4217
www.xulonpress.com

A note to churches, ministries, and bookstores: **Quantity discounts** will be applied to all multiple orders. For your discount offer, please contact us at

Safe Harbor Ministry
P.O. Box 456
Toms River, NJ 08754
safeharborministry@comcast.net
www.safeharborministry.org

Printed in the United States of America

Paperback ISBN-13: 978-1-6312-9622-2
Ebook ISBN-13: 978-1-6312-9623-9

Why I Shout: Thirty-One Reasons to Rejoice in the Lord;
A month of meditations for your daily journey to freedom
By Sharon Nzwalla Ryan with Christopher Capen Ryan

This book is dedicated to the Lord Jesus Christ,
To Whom I give all of my shouts!

And to my husband, Christopher,
without whom this book would not have been written

TABLE OF CONTENTS

FOREWORD

THOMAS WESLEY WEEKS, SR.

I am going to preface my comments by asserting that we were all created to know the true and living God. It is the very purpose of our existence. Sharon Nzwalla Ryan's **Why I Shout** is a "once upon a time" story with evidence proving me correct. Humanity's history is filled with millions of recorded, evidence-based stories. But Sharon's story is about someone I've been privileged to know for twenty-five years. **Why I Shout** tracks her upside-down life, which, all of a sudden, gets flipped to a "right-side-up life." Here's a "believe it or not" story of why Sharon shouts! Of how she came to know the true and living God. As you read along, you may remember or discover something in your own life, giving you reason to shout. (I can think of one reason — and that is, you've been through some stuff in your own life <u>and</u> you're still alive!) You are alive to know your Creator. Regardless of your past, He is alive to help you navigate the rest of your life. The rest of your life will really be worth shouting about.

We thank Sharon for showing us that our life stories can become embedded in God and His life principles. May we all harness these God principles. As we follow Sharon, we may discover some things to shout about in our own lives. Let's let our shouts out; let them rise to the very heavens!

I say to you, reader, let's praise the Lord as we shout along with Sharon.

Thomas Wesley Weeks, Sr.

NOW A NOTE FROM SHARON TO HER SPIRITUAL FATHER, APOSTLE THOMAS W. WEEKS, SR.

"You have the title of Apostle [this word comes from the Greek *apostolo* and means "builder"]. You lead; you build in your sphere of influence to build up the Church, so as to shape the world for God's purposes. For me, the word *apostolo* has a special meaning. When I sojourned in Wilmington, Delaware for those seven years under your watchful eye and encouraging tutelage, you built me up; you "apostled" me. And here in 2020, as I revisit and revise and restructure **Why I Shout**, I am standing on solid ground, built up in Christ with you helping to build me up along the way. Thank you, Apostle-Dad!

—Sharon

A NOTE FROM CHRISTOPHER

I met Sharon back in the winter of 1991. We scarcely knew each other when I eventually invited her to go out for lunch. I remember sitting across the table from her and out of the blue, I declared that she would write a book someday. Sharon asked me what it would be called. Without any hesitation I said, "Why I Shout"!

Where did that bold prediction come from? I had nothing really substantive to go on. I knew a bit of her dramatic story. It was in the next nine months after that lunch, leading up to our marriage, that I found out about her life. You see, Sharon was not shy about telling me about her prior addicted, hopeless existence. Sharon gave all the credit to God for her dramatic rescue. Sharon had become a lover of Christ, a follower of Christ, and she loved telling about her faith in her Rescuer.

I had first seen Sharon "shouting" her faith in a church gathering; a new face and a lively presence on the Sunday morning worship team. This team had always been spirited in their praises to God, but with the recent addition of Sharon to the team, I wondered, "Who is this loud, wild woman?" Three weeks later, Sharon and I actually met at a Christian singles gathering, which, as it turned out, neither of us had really wanted to attend. I saw her sitting with some other women and when she got up, I happened to be right in her path. I felt a little awkward but ventured a "hello" and introduced myself. We ended up talking for a while. Her life story lined up with her Sunday morning congregational worship. I silently concluded, "Hmmm, a strong faith-sister." It was one Sunday after church that I went up to her and blurted out, "Do you want go for some Chinese lunch?" Two hours into our lunch together, I made my declaration about the yet-to-be book, **Why I Shout**.

Our paths didn't cross again for several weeks. I was more interested in skiing and teaching skiing than attending church. And I had no romantic leanings toward Sharon (yet!)

Then one day, Sharon called me to ask for some assistance writing a cover letter for her resume. During that luncheon together, I had mentioned my years of teaching writing skills. (The weird thing - I found out later that Sharon had taught resume and cover letter writing herself. But when it came to writing her own cover letter, she contracted writer's cramp) I reluctantly agreed to take a look at her cover letter project. My whole life, at that time, was in such a funk that I didn't believe I could be of much help. As it turned out, while we were working on the letter, she turned out to be a tremendous help to me. In the midst of me interviewing her, I told Sharon of my life woes. She patiently listened and then prayed with me, later declaring that I would teach again, even though I had just told her, "I'll never teach again." (I started a new teaching job less than a year later, right after we had married!)

Well, I completed the cover letter after two evenings of interviewing and getting to know each other. At 2am on the second evening, I fell in love with Sharon; but she had no clue. I didn't let on to my romantic implosion. I awkwardly made my way to the door, simply saying, "Good night." Come to find out days later, Sharon had been left wondering about my abrupt exit, "This guy is kind of strange!" Three months later, I proposed marriage, and several months later, our wedding! Sharon was shouting long before meeting me and she hasn't stopped shouting in the almost-thirty years that we've been married. The pages to follow are our collaborative writing effort. Sharon dear, it's been exciting working with you on this book. I love you.

—Your husband

ACKNOWLEDGEMENTS

This has been the rewarding part of writing *Why I Shout,* remembering the so many people along my life's path who have helped get me to the shouting. They have encouraged me, exhorted me, corrected me, and even rebuked me. Where would I be had they not been in my life? I will mention those I presently can call to mind. I hope I didn't leave anyone out; but if you are reading this and you know that you belong in the following list, pen your name in and contact me.

Millie Mitchell, what you went through even before I was born, and then when you delivered me to life, you had your hands full with sensitive me. My babyhood, my childhood, my early teen years. OYYY! Thanks, Mom. Thank you, Arthur Mitchell, for co-partnering in the making of my body/soul. You, Anthony Anderson, my son, have no idea! You, big guy, at eighteen years old, confronted me, "Ma, you need some help!" I was in denial and told you, "Get out of my face; go on, up to school." I thought I didn't need any help when, truth be told, I was habitually so high or drunk I could scarcely find my way home at night. On that same day after your admonition, "Go see the new pastor up at church," I went up to that church.

And you, Dr. Donald Hilliard, greeted me as I showed up — unannounced, unknown to you. You invited me in; you offered me your hospitable heart. You proceeded to open the way to beginning my new life; you guided me to Jesus as my Savior. Minister Phyllis Hilliard, you were warmly encouraging, as I toddled through my early Christian growth. Karol Grier, thank you for nurturing me and holding my hand through those first years of my life in the Lord.

How could I ever forget that day when you stopped by my house? I was about to be tempted beyond my own strength. As that fast-talking man made his way into my apartment, and trotted out his marijuana and wine on my living room table, I was silently pleading with God, *"Get this man out of here"*. Then you knocked on my door. He took one look at you, packed up his "bait," and scrammed. Whew! Denise Graham, thank you for coming to visit me, over and over again. You were there for me in my growing pains as I was living this born-again life. Charles Singletary, thanks for being an uncommon brother. Pastor David Trawick, what a godly benefactor in my struggling, single-mothering days. Charles Johnson, an-out-of-the-box, crazy brother! You made me laugh and light up. Bishop Leroy Holmes, you spent five years mentoring and grooming me for kingdom warfare in the world of prisons, jails, and inmate reentry to society. Although you came at me like a drill sergeant, I thank you for the tough love. You said I needed some thick skin. Thanks for the callouses. I would need them later in life, dealing with rejection and confrontation. Elizabeth Phifer, you gave me a place to stay when I had nowhere to go, and you made me feel at home with your unconditional love. Jim and Beverly Spence, you allowed me to spread my wings when you hired me as a counselor into your halfway house in the faraway state of Massachusetts. Rebecca Simmons, in the winter of 2003-2004 you acted as a pre-midwife, coaxing me to keep on gestating "baby book".

Enter Pneuma Books in 2004, enabling us to publish the first edition of **Why I Shout**. Those sweltering summer days with the Pneuma team of Brian Taylor and Nina Groop Taylor, as well as Mike Morris, wrestling the manuscript, layout and design into publication readiness. Sixteen years ago, that was some design, editing, and layout. Page Hatcher, you nailed it with that quintessential portrait featured on the original back jacket-cover. Finally, a huge 2020 hurrah to Xulon Press for this "second generation" version of **Why I Shout.** We don't know everyone on your team, but we recognize James Matthes for diplomatically "recruiting" us to go with Xulon when we were shopping for a full-service Author group. Kim Small, as our Author Rep, you triaged us week after week, month after month, through the publication process. Most importantly, I acknowledge You, Lord Jesus Christ, for giving me Your life, and then for "putting my life out there" in this book as a testimony to Your goodness and faithfulness. Where would I be without You?! You are the reason I shout.

IN THE BEGINNING

Why I Shout has been in the making since 1984. In fact, February 15, 1984 marked the first day of the "rough-drafting process." My shouting began on that special day, but it took me many years to actually start writing some of the "shout thoughts" on paper. The original book came out in 2004. With this edition of 2020, you'll find lots of new "shout thoughts" that have become "printed thoughts". We've created a whole new feature, called **Prompts,** where you'll find invitations and opportunities for you, the reader, to reflect and write your own thoughts!

On that day, after Valentine's Day 1984, I woke up, as usual, a functioning addict. The path to addiction had begun nearly twenty years before. But on February 15, 1984, for the first time in twenty years, I went to bed in my right mind never to do drugs or drink again. The pages you are about to read will give you some snapshots of my crazy, wonderful story. These pages point to the One who has enabled me to live a life of thirty-six years in one hundred percent recovery from addiction. And while there have been other areas of my life that have needed a change for the better, I have come to experience change in those areas. You, dear reader, may want to experience some change in an area of your own life. Read on with me and learn to believe that "all things are possible with the One"[1] who is lovingly available to come alongside you on your life journey.

You have a history that is still in the making. Before creating more of your history, have you ever thought about taking an intentional look at your issues, your "stuff"? The interactive questions and prompts **at the end of each chapter** may help you begin tracking your issues, your stuff, and your story. How about keeping a journal (or a voice-recorder) to respond to the questions and prompts? Your responses, in turn, may find you "streaming" your story; blooming into a book; launching a blog; writing to all your close family, or alienated family. And if you are key-boarding or penciling for your own benefit, give no thought to grammar or spelling. In whatever way you respond to the prompts, remember, this is your adventure; for your eyes or ears only, if that is what you choose. Do not even think about what anyone else might think if you choose to keep it private. And if you get stuck and don't know what to write, know that even the most successful writers and authors experience writer's cramp. They freeze up. Do what they do, don't retreat – take a break, then write, even if it is bit by bit; here-a-day, there-a-day. Just do it, and you'll discover things about your past and your present that will give you something to shout about along the way.

*Now I who was once **out of it altogether** — am in on everything!*
Ephesians 2:12, The Message

<u>Prompt</u>: We all have areas of our lives where we are "out of it altogether." We all have stuff. Take a moment to start recognizing those areas in your journal.

> <u>A note from Sharon</u> — Don't be dis-heartened if the process of journaling is sometimes uncomfortable. Remember, the context of the above verse from Ephesians. There is a transformative work Christ can work in our "out of it altogether" stuff. Transforming is no biggie for the Creator of the universe. He will

put us "in on everything."; help us in every area of our lives. Discover the "everything" pathway, laid out in the entire second chapter of Ephesians (which is found in the New Testament part of the Scriptures). This "everything" verse is taken from The Message (a marvelously written, twenty-first century, paraphrased rendering of the Bible. Available electronically at the App.store or in print version) If I had to choose one version of the Bible to pack for my next trip to Texas or to Africa, I would bring the Spirit-Filled Life Bible, a comprehensive study Bible. You may choose from one of several different translations: New King James Version or the New Living Translation or the New International Version. I recommend the Spirit-Filled Life Bible in the NKJV translation, which is known for its adherence to the original languages and its contextual accuracy. The Passion Translation of the Bible came out in recent years and is touted as a version that "will help you encounter God's heart and discover what He has for your life." For sure the language of TPT is passionate and accurate. Although not all of the sixty-six books are available yet, it is a version that will put a new vitality in your reading and studying of the greatest and most read book of all time.

AS YOU LEAD ME

On February 15, 1984, I learned there was a God who cared about messed-up me. My life had been out of control for years. That day, after an early breakfast of several Heinekens, topped off with a deep smoke of marijuana, my eighteen-year-old son came into my bedroom, "You need some help, Ma. There's this cool new pastor up there at the church on Broad Street." My push-back response, "Get out of here; go to school." Two hours later, I found myself sitting in the parsonage of that old church with a young pastor, who was new to my hometown of Perth Amboy, New Jersey. Pastor Donald Hilliard listened to my story. Right there, in that moment, my hopeless life flashed before me. "Sharon, you've tried just about everything under the sun. How about trying Jesus?" I don't remember what the pastor said next. All I know is I started crying and saying, "Yes, yes, I want Jesus to come for me."

Then Pastor Hilliard led me in three verbal declarations, leading me to Jesus. Declaration one: "I have made a mess of my life; Jesus, please forgive me for all my wrong-doing, my sins." Second: "I need You to save me from myself, from the devil, from eternal death, and hell. I need You to guide me 24/7/365. So, Holy Spirit, please come; be my Spirit-guide." Third, just like I used to do when the police pulled me over, I put my hands up in surrender (usually I'd place them on top of the car roof or hood). Now I was surrendering to Jesus, declaring that He is Lord (meaning not only am I saved, but I give my life-living over to His way, will, and purpose). Then I cried and laughed hysterically. The pastor's wife, Phyllis, and their three young daughters rushed in to see what all the commotion was about. They prayed with me, and then Phyllis grabbed me by my hands and started dancing me around the parsonage with the three little girls in tow. I hugged the Hilliards and made my way home. What had happened? I marveled at how now I had no desire to get drunk or high. I laid my head down on my pillow that night. What a first night of my born-again, God-interrupted life!

Since then, I have been learning to let God be involved in every aspect of my life. Letting go of me and letting Him take me over has been an ongoing struggle and, at the same time, the foundation for the "me-in-Jesus" life. Over the years, I have been challenged in my single-ness, in my marriage (to Christopher), in all of my relationships, and even in my obedience to God. Will I have things my way or will I let Him direct me in His way?

I am always facing new opportunities to apply the basic truth that I have learned from the Master: "I will lead you, Sharon, with My eye" (Psalm 32:8). This promise is for you too. Insert your own name in there, or you may flip that to say, "Lord, You will lead me with Your eye."

To follow the Leader has been a life pursuit — through starts and stops, faltering and falling, fits and failure. I have learned over and over again that He is intimately involved and concerned with me; that He promises to never leave me or let me down. And yet, I must admit that I have been through many times of doubt and despair, to the point of wondering whether God was really leading me at all. Each time of doubting and fearing, I came to find out He was still there and leading me. Will I let Him continue to lead me?

God can do anything, you know ... not by pushing us around
but by working within us, his Spirit deeply and gently within us.
Ephesians 3:20, The Message

<u>Prompt:</u> Do you sense that there is **something** you know **you just have to do**? That may be for you who loves God, the Spirit of God is at work in your spirit. Someone would insist that's really just your conscience. Be that as it may, you know you to have to take a stance on a tough issue; or you may have to make a tough decision to bring some change into your own life. Possibly a relationship needs tending to. Let Him lead you. Just do it!

DO I TRUST HIM?

Twila Paris's piercing song "Do I Trust You?"[2] addresses the most basic issue of life. (Do you know that trusting God has been humanity's fundamental challenge ever since Adam and Eve?) I was a single mom (and a failure at that) when I called out to God, and He responded as mighty life Saver, rescuing me from drugs and alcohol. Then He started to school me in His ways — ways that I found totally contrary to my street ways, my tough-girl smarts. Even though I now had my new life in Jesus, I was still on welfare. I had started to attend Sunday morning church and, thanks to Pastor Hilliard's Sunday teachings, I came to hear that God asks His followers to give ten percent (a tithe) of their income to His work. So, from that meager monthly welfare check, I faithfully set aside ten percent of my welfare check to put in the Sunday offering basket. That kind of budget allotment made no sense to this welfare mom.

When I decided to obey His command to give that tithe, following through came easily. In His enabling grace, I gave. In a few months, I was off welfare; I was hired as a landlord-tenant counselor, a position that I had no training for. According to "the system," I certainly did not qualify. However, I believe my new job came from God's hand at work in the Human Resources office. From receiving welfare to providing counsel to tenants with landlord issues; a breakthrough that could only be attributed to God's favor and faithfulness!

BTW: In 2020, I now see tithing in a whole different light — the Old Testament law compared with the liberty and grace proclaimed in the New Testament. Tithing in the Old Testament days was a benchmark of meeting the requirements of the law. Jesus fulfilled and satisfied those requirements of the Law when He put His sinless, perfect life on the Cross. When we follow Jesus's command to love God with all our hearts and to love our neighbor as ourselves, then giving our time, our talents, and our money are expressions of His sons' and daughters' love for Him. And that may mean giving ten percent of my income (or more). And while you may be grappling with this whole concept of giving a full ten percent, you may start out by giving less! It's a heart thing. Let Him and you be partners in this whole realm of how much to give to Your Provider's kingdom work here on earth. What will that look like? Hopefully you have a church or you'll find a church, a ministry, a Gospel-centered gathering where your giving will be like planting seeds in good soil. The soil of God's work tended to by God-honoring leaders, pastors, or ministers. And you'll have a part in that by being connected and learning and growing in the things of God. And most importantly, growing in your relationship with God the Father, Jesus the Son of God, and the Spirit of God!

In subsequent seasons of my life, I have had to wait and trust, trust and wait. I've waited for new jobs. I waited for my husband-to-be. The waiting can be agonizing. *"Are you sure You've got me, Lord?"* Or *"Don't You think you're running a little late, God?"* And I've even shouted, "What is going on here?" These were my very plain questions. Yes, sometimes I freaked out. How could my Father look on me when I nursed these all-too-human attitudes? But then I asked myself, *Isn't the Lord to be trusted with our attitudes as well as our lives?* Google that song, "Do I Trust You, Lord?" (and make sure it's the version sung by Twila Paris).

Trust God from the bottom of your heart;
don't try to figure out everything on your own.
Listen for God's voice in everything you do,
everywhere you go; He's the One who will keep you on track.

Don't assume that you know it all. Run to God! Run from evil!
Proverbs 3:5-7, The Message

<u>Prompt:</u> In what challenging life situations are you most likely to try and figure it out on your own?

<u>Option A</u> <<**On your own**>>-How is that working for you? Have you found it to be a reliable "go-to"? I think not! This is the old Adam-Eve paradigm. The two of them in the Garden decided to do life without God.

<u>Option B</u> <<**Living in and through Jesus, listening to Holy Spirit's voice**>>. This is a trust-dynamic, allowing you to bypass your limited self (and to resist the Devil's demonic agents). Pay special attention to Ephesians 6:10-18, particularly in <u>The Message</u> translation, for a strategy to resist our enemy. Read the Scriptures, asking the Spirit of God to show you how to apply them to your life! The truths of Scripture wrapped with Holy Spirit's leading - a <u>G</u>od <u>P</u>ositioning <u>S</u>ystem for you. He is the GPS; you are a pilgrim, a way-farer. Hey, trekker-girl, tundra-man! Let the Spirit flow within your core, routing you and re-routing you through every turn of the Way. When you are not sure of your next move, calm yourself. The Most High One will not leave you hanging, because your Creator is trust-worthy! And when you're really at a loss to find your way, He will use whatever it takes to get you back with Him and on track.

It may be an experienced follower of Christ to come alongside you to provide wise counsel. A listening ear/heart to your thinking-out-loud; a "yes" nod toward your hunch; an answer to your question; reassurance in the midst of your doubts and fears; resolution for your pending decision, even if it means a "no way." In all the squirrely-ness of your Jesus life, don't get it twisted! You are not alone; you are not deficient; you are not weird. All of Christ's followers, including Martin Luther, Mother Theresa, and Martin

Luther King Jr. have gone through the valley of doubts, fears, and tough decisions. Be encouraged, knowing that you, as a believer and follower of Jesus, have been saved from the Enemy! **Why**? Because God wants us all to live as His own daughters and sons, listening to Him, living in Him, and living for Him.

AND AGAIN I ASK, DO I TRUST HIM?

My friend was vehement. "Get dressed; we're going to the emergency room!" Frances was not playing; I knew that I'd better go along with her. But in the back of my mind, I was thinking, *Okay, God, I don't feel well but I refuse to go to the doctor.*

I had only known the Lord for less than a year, and I had heard that Jesus heals. I didn't realize that I had to take care of my body to co-operate with His health plan. I had been a drug addict, and I didn't know how to give my body the special care it needed after so many years of drug abuse. Not only was I not taking vitamins and minerals, but I was attracted to salty, oily foods and lots of chocolate cake. I gained fifty pounds after I stopped doing drugs. At the emergency room, I learned my sugar level read 420+ (stroke range). The doctor announced that I actually could have died had I not listened to Francis.

"You are not going back to your apartment; we are signing you into a room immediately." I was devastated. What about my faith? Hadn't I been trusting my Savior to take care of me? After all, He had rescued me from cocaine, pills, and heroin. Now I had diabetes? Why did I come so close to death? "Do You really care for me, God?"

The medical center cared for me in those days of doubt and questioning. God used the staff to tell me that I would have to learn how to eat right to control the diabetes. When I heard I would be on insulin for the rest of my life, something rose up on the inside. "No way, Lord; You did not deliver me from the heroin needle to now have me dependent on the insulin needle four times a day."

Thirty-five years have come and gone in quest of stable blood sugar levels through intentionally balancing my intake of food, medication, and natural supplements; seasons of disciplined lifestyle, thrown off by a week or two of fried chicken and potato-chip binging; every couple of years ending up in the ER and having to resume insulin injections, not to mention blood pressure medication. Then my natural practitioner, Doctor Natalia from Russia, tells me, "Yah, so now I retire, yes." What now? Who can I trust with my health care? My friend, Dottie Scalzo, suggested, "Sharon, you just have to meet my doctor." Christmas Eve 2018, at three-thirty pm, I was sitting in front of Dr. Vladamir Berkovich (another Russian) who ordered a fourteen-page blood panel. Three weeks later, I came back for a follow-up consultation. His prognosis called for a holistic regimen of prescribed pharmaceuticals and alternative supplements. A year later, I was down to a single, tiny night-time dose of a new type of slow-release insulin. No longer in the diabetic range, and now with normal blood pressure for the first time in thirty years, I am shouting with gratitude and amazement. Thank God for the turnaround; I thank God for Dr. Berkovich. Dottie, you get some credit too, girl! Whatever my state of health, I want to continue to trust God.

Trust in the Lord, and do good; dwell in the land,
and feed on His faithfulness. Delight yourself also
in the Lord, and He will give you the desires of your heart.
Psalm 37:3-4, NKJV

Prompt : Can you imagine that His faithfulness has the power to actually transform your heart and mind, to rearrange your very desires?

For reflection: Your cooperation with His Spirit at work within you will find you discovering your "new real you", your God-created God-transformed self! You'll begin to harmonize with His best for you. And that may mean what you used to desire will no longer be tugging at your heart strings. Your past with its hurts, disappointments, failures, and sin "informed" a lot of those old desires and decisions. Now, as a follower of Jesus, your past sins don't count. They don't inform anything. Through His sacrificial death on the Cross, your sin is forgiven and your soul is being healed. Watch how your old desires begin to "not count" either! Change becomes your daily norm, as you see how your life is being worked out here on earth. After thirty years of diabetes, controlled by several injections of insulin a day, a major desire of my heart was satisfied. In 2018, I encountered my God-sent doctor and my God-fueled compliance with his radical medical paradigm, which resulted in *voila* – the desire of my heart finally got realized. I am out of the diabetic range, and I no longer depend on several doses of insulin to get through the day.

YOU'VE GOT A PLAN, I'VE GOT A PURPOSE

★ ★ ★

I was on a bus to Massachusetts. I wasn't excited about leaving my familiar hometown surroundings in New Jersey to go for a job interview in cold New England. My mentor, Pastor Leroy Holmes, had put the bus fare in my hand and exhorted me to go. "Sister Sharon, don't let people, places, or things ever stop you from doing what God says." For five years I had been shadowing Pastor Holmes; he regularly took me into a half-dozen prisons and jails. He had a God-story to tell the inmates — he had served time for second degree murder as a Mafia debt collector. I had learned how to carry myself with poise and confidence – thanks to his experience and wisdom. Little did I realize I was being trained to step into the front lines of the penal system – without him! Here I was on my way to the faith-based Bridge House in Framingham, Massachusetts. The position? Counseling paroled male felons, most of them recovering addicts.

The house director, Rev. Jim Spence, met me at the bus terminal and took me to meet his wife, Bev. They had a guest room prepared for me in their cozy Colonial-style home. We settled down to dinner and then talked for hours about the halfway house and the mission there. Jim and Bev were warm, open, and seemed to like me. The next morning, Jim came thundering down the stairs, "God told me during the night that you are the one for this job." Smarty-mouth me wanted to say, "Oh, yeah, how come He didn't consult with me first?" I could scarcely believe what I was hearing. We went through the formality of an interview. I was now Counselor Sharon.

Where was I going to live, and how was I going to get to work? I had absolutely no money to put down on an apartment, and I didn't own a car. Well, it just so happened that a nearby attic apartment was up for rent. Now, how to pay? Bev offered to advance the first month's rent and security. I could walk to work. Within twenty-four hours of arriving for my Massachusetts interview, I had a job and an apartment. I was a sure-enough believer! Right there in that little New England town, God started to unfold His plan and my purpose. I had been called to help set these men free.

For I know the plans [and purposes] I have for you
Jeremiah 29:11, NLT

Prompt: Do you know your purpose/purposes? Can you accept that there is a God who has a plan for your life?

How do your will and your availability play a part in that purpose and plan being fulfilled?

WHY ME? WHY HERE? WHY NOW?

These were the questions I had wrestled with on the bus, as I went to that interview in Massachusetts. Those questions were answered. I came to know that God had sent me to the Bridge House. He had hand-picked me to work with those dysfunctional men (and their damaged families).

So I wasn't exactly ready for the pink slip a year into my work at the halfway house. Wasn't I chosen by the Lord Himself to counsel these guys? What will they do without me? What will I do without a pay-check? These were natural questions. State parole funding had been cut, and downsizing struck the Bridge House. I was the newest hire, so I was the first to be cut. *Why me, God? You have just brought me here. And now are you abandoning me? Lord, don't forget I don't have Plan B here in Massachusetts.*

Actually, I came to see later that the "why me, why here, why now" can be appropriate questions to ask God in every season and every change in life. In fact, I don't think He minds us questioning Him at all. Aren't we His children, and don't children ask such questions?

The Bible says, "All things work together for good to those who love God and are called according to His purpose" (Romans 8:28). Behind all of life's changes and seasons, there must be purpose and reason. I don't pretend to understand it all. Yet, I still like to ask God, *What's up?*

As it turned out, I had to go on unemployment compensation for nearly a year. I watched the Lord supply my every need; I was able to pay every bill. In the midst of waiting on God for my next assignment, God allowed me to ask lots of questions, even though He didn't always give me an answer. I was learning to trust Him in the midst of all my questions. Surely He had the answers to "Why me? Why here? Why now?"

My future is in your hands Psalm 31:15, NLT

<u>Prompt</u>: Do you have a "<u>Why me, why here, why now?</u>" story?

What "season" of your life are you in right now?

What questions do you ponder about your future? (Please, no abstract generalizations; no "holy pie" in the sky! Get real. Get concrete.)

AT LAST, I HAVE A HUSBAND

I had been with many men, but none had ever really cared for me. (And now I know I wasn't able to really care for any one of them either.) They all left me, and I felt betrayed and desperate. I was going to bed lonely and waking up lonely. When I met with Pastor Hilliard on that providential February 15, 1984, he had pointed me to Jesus as my only hope in my loneliness. Jesus, he said, could be my husband. As I returned to my apartment on that winter day in 1984, I didn't mind the cold weather. I knew I was on my way home to my new Husband. And I knew I had to "clean house" to make it suitable for Him.

I was exhilarated as I opened my door. I immediately threw all my drugs and alcohol in the trash. I no longer needed those sub-stances to fill the void in my love-starved life. I felt as if Jesus Himself had accompanied me home. Out of the blue, I started singing, "Jesus, be a fence all around me." I was high on Jesus. At that moment, I figured I could live the rest of my life without a man. After all, men only wanted to use me and then leave me. Just me and Jesus; that would be just fine. Pastor Hilliard had pro-claimed Jesus will never change His love toward me.

Seven years later, a good man came into my life. I am now mar-ried to that good man, Christopher. He is my God-sent, not my God. In our nearly thirty years of marriage, I have come to know him in all his humanity. I find myself wrestling with his limitations and my expectations. And usually I'll end up allowing the Spirit of the Living God to remind me that Jesus is my perfect Man. In Paul's letter to the Ephesians in the Bible, Christ is portrayed as

Bridegroom. So, that makes Him my heavenly husband! We as His followers, female and male, are His Bride and live in an eternal marriage covenant. Here on earth, I live in marital covenant with Christopher. I respect him as my husband (most of the time — LOL); I purpose to love him as my husband, but I must look to Jesus as my ultimate husband. Christopher cares for me, but only Jesus, my Bridegroom, is able to care for me perfectly.

Christ cares for His body
[this is a paraphrase of Ephesians 5:29-30, which portrays us followers of Christ as members or parts of His body, the worldwide body of His believers.]

<u>Prompt</u>: Do you experience Jesus as your husband?

Do you know Him intimately? Have you a sense that Christ cares for you; that He actually takes care of you?

ALONE, NOT LONELY

Though I grew up in a family with a mother, a father, and an older sister, I always felt lonely. Oh, we ate meals together, went to church together, and took vacations together. My mother didn't know my love language. She would buy me shoes and make sure I was well dressed. Good manners – no problem! I knew them all. Hugs and words of encouragement or comfort were few and far between. My father lived under the same roof with us, but seldom spoke to me. He went to work every day and read the paper every evening. My older sister was in her own world; it just looked different from mine. When I was in my teens, I left home to find approval and affection from guys. Not a wise solution for my lonely life, as it took me twenty years of guy-hopping and guy-using to realize that men were not a solution to my loneliness.

When I asked Jesus into my heart on that day after Valentine's Day, I began to experience "another world" – *What is this?* I knew it was a God-thing; love and acceptance flooded over me. Mysterious, but I knew beyond a shadow of a doubt that my loneliness was fading away. And as I began to explore His wonderful Book, I encountered a curious statement that seemed to contradict my life story. "God places the lonely in families" (Psalm 68:6). I thought, *Lord, I know You've given me good brothers and sisters in the church, but I don't feel like I grew up as part of a family.* Since meeting God on Valentine's Day 1984, I had begun to call Him my Father, my Brother, my Sister, and my Mother. But at times, I still wished I had a family here on earth to visit and love. Then it happened — I had moved to Massachusetts to answer God's call. I found a church I could call my own. A matronly woman whom I used to see every

Sunday came up to me one morning, "You need a mother." Hope embraced me with her bosomy hug. Never, ever had I felt this deep acceptance. I was at her home for Sunday dinners, weekday suppers, and family holidays. "You don't have a proper bed, dear?" Hope made sure I got a proper bed. I became her daughter. Those two years with Momma Hope before I married Christopher gave me a family experience. Twelve years later, another family halfway around the world became my family! You will read of my adoptive East African family in Chapter 9. Twenty years have passed since our ministry-*safari* (trip) to Mwanza, Tanzania. And now after all of those Jesus-borne years of "family-replacement therapy" both in the USA and in Africa, I relish my solitude.

I've embraced my "new-normal" introvert self. I am happy to spend days on end without going outside of our home. It's me and my husband (whenever he comes in from his marketplace ministry). I'm in my seventies now; I've out-grown that chronic loneliness of my first thirty-six years on the planet. While I know I'm bound for my Father's house in the kingdom of God, I find myself at home in this human vessel of spirit, soul, and body. No longer lonely; home alone with Jesus is alright with me. <u>Christopher's Disclaimer</u>: In the course of some weeks, Sharon may log a total of twenty to thirty hours of screen time/phone time. Does that qualify her as a "virtual extrovert"? Well, most of that time is Kingdom time, not *coffee klatch* time. Sharing; counseling, discipling. Surfing the web for spiritual growth and development. Content, solo, intro. Invigorating, sharing extro .

God places the lonely in families. Psalm 68:6, NLT

Beginning here with Chapter 8, you will find that not every chapter has a concluding Prompt. But you'll be able to access additional prompts on www.safeharborministry.org

I WAS ADOPTED

As a fifth-grader, I actually told God that I felt gypped because I had no brothers to grow up with. Little did I know that as a fully grown, fifty-five-year-old woman, I would be adopted into a whole family of six brothers. Bishop Robert Nzwalla and his wife Irene had been invited to America to raise support for their churches in Tanzania. One weekend, their hosting pastor from Virginia scholar-shipped them to a marriage seminar in rural Pennsylvania. Christopher and I were there too, on that providential breakfast morning. "Honey, could I please have the butter?" Our neighboring table couple overheard me, and the husband queried, "Excuse me; where are you from?" I responded," Delaware." Our table neighbor exclaimed, "My wife and I had just been thinking that you are of the Maasai tribe in eastern Africa and your husband a European. But when I heard you ask for the butter, I tell my wife, 'Oh, no! She is from here.'" We became instant friends, the four of us laughing about the butter conversation. At the conclusion of the weekend, we drove the Nzwallas back to Virginia.

A week later, Robert called us, "Maybe you could help us; Irene's sister has just died from malaria. She must go home to bury her." Irene flew home, and then we were able to host Robert on several weekends at our home in Delaware. "You must come to Mwanza, Tanzania in April and inaugurate our pastors' training school. And I tell you, I have just talked on the phone with my brother at home in Africa. I tell him, 'I have just met our new sister in America. We must adopt her into our family when she comes!'"

Seven months later, we flew into Kenya. Robert met us at the airport and drove us sixteen hours to his home in Tanzania. Everything was new: the language, the food, and all of my family-to-be. I was so excited I could scarcely contain myself. Saturday came and preparations for the adoption ceremony got underway. The women of the family spent the whole day in the courtyard outside of my window, preparing the feast. Late in the afternoon, Irene finally appeared in my room to dress me in Kikuyu tribal garb. Like a bride walking down the aisle on her wedding day, I was ushered into the great family room where all eyes were upon me.

Speeches and blessings abounded as the adoption ceremony unfolded. Hugs and tears; then came the call to feast. Two goats had been slaughtered, and the meat was mingled together to represent the joining of the two families. We ate heartily and joyfully in celebration.

That adoption meal of freshly slaughtered goat reminded me that Jesus had been slaughtered for me. Because of His spilled blood, I am part of His family. And daily I celebrate that I am in His family forever. Thank You, Father, for sending Jesus so that I could be adopted!

His unchanging plan has always been
to adopt us into His family
by sending Jesus Christ to die for us.
And He did this because He wanted to.
Ephesians 1:5, The Living Bible

<u>Prompt:</u> Introvert or extrovert, how do you experience you being part of the Jesus family? (And we're not talking about just church gatherings; how about home gatherings; virtual gatherings; correspondence; phone calls?)

How does God's unchanging plan offset the pain of strained or alienated relationships? How about not growing up in a healthy family environment?

Or, perhaps you grew up in a good family environment. Realizing that no family is perfect, what possible lack may be "waiting" for you to "resolve" in the perfecting adoption of God's family? Ask the Spirit to guide you into this exploration.

10

CONTENTMENT

You would think I should be pretty content. I have my husband and I have Jesus. And then again, it's really Jesus and Christopher — in that order. But I still have more to learn about practical contentment with daily living. We've been in our new home for five years — a condo we didn't pay for. Bought for us, cash — the gift of a couple who know our ministry, who love us, and desired to bless us (without anyone but us knowing). For the first time in our lives, we own a home with no mortgage payments. But have I really been content?

I mean, it's just one bedroom and I'd like to have a guest bedroom; and a larger family room so we could host fellowship gatherings. I've been imagining a new look for our kitchen cabinets. What if we removed the worn 1970s linoleum floors in the kitchen and long hallway? Not so long ago, I even started to consider selling our condo and upscaling! That whole thought came to an abrupt halt when we were told by a realtor that all the 55+ senior dwellings in our village association must be paid for in full. No mortgages??! That helped me address the real meaning of contentment.

We are not even wanting to revisit the burden of monthly mortgage payments, thank God! And then it was as though I heard the Lord say, "So, you want to have another home?" I have decided if another dwelling is in store for us, it will be the doing of our Provider — no doubt about it — and without a mortgage.

Over the years, I have struggled with the whole issue of contentment. I know that Hebrews 13:5 admonishes us to be content with what we have. I have not always been satisfied, but the Holy Spirit has a way of counseling me (here am I, myself a counselor!). Mighty Counselor is counseling me in the process of being grateful and content — even with our worn floors and aged cabinet doors.

Be relaxed with what you have.
Hebrews 13:5, The Message

<u>Prompt:</u> Paul, in the book of Philippians, spoke of his enduring contentment — in his former days of ample freedom and provision, and then in the deprivation of his jail cell. Paul had *learned* to be content.

Reflect on your contentment dynamic.

In what areas of your life (both outward and within) are you relaxed with what you have? How about any area of discontent?

CREATIVITY

Me, creative? No way, I used to think! But then I remember coming home after school. No one else was home yet! I had my make-believe mic, and I was Diana Ross – all 112 lbs. of my bean-pole, tenth-grade self. My mother would be coming in from work around 4pm. So I had an hour to indulge my Motown fantasy. Yes, I would be the next Diana Ross...until four pm when I would take up my quiet, book-studying persona, behind the shut door of my bedroom. My mother was bent on her dream of me being her teacher-daughter, Sharon Mitchell. My mother, Millie Belle Mitchell, was well-meaning, but I now know she herself had wanted to go to college and become a teacher. Her mother, Alberta Barrigher, squashed that dream. "Ain't gonna have no daughter of mine waste no time and good money taking up college when she can get a good job."

My grandmother had grown up in the twilight years of share-cropping in Albany, Georgia. She and her daughter came north where jobs were plentiful and money was to be made. World War II found her in Bristol, Pennsylvania, making military coats for troops in wintry Europe. But the soul-battle in the Barrigher family was to make something out of life, to make some cash money, and hopefully to own a house. My mother grew up benefiting materially from her mother's drive, and now she was going to make sure that I had the benefit of a college education. I was going to be my mother's dream, a teacher.

At sixteen, I ran away from home. The next twenty years passed, as an alcohol/drug-based flight from the pain of my repressed, abusive childhood. But all was not lost. In 1984, my creativity began to come uncapped as I came to Jesus; I sang to Jesus in the shower. Years later, I married Christopher. We own a condo. I sense great pleasure in re-decorating and re-arranging our living space. Our entire home is a tapestry of color and texture. My husband calls me "the Martha Stewart that never went to prison." I spontaneously dance my shouts to my Creator in congregational worship meetings. I am constantly journaling. I've birthed a book; you're reading it! I can now say I am expressing my creativity. "Yay" for creativity. Diana Ross, thank you. I am doing creative me!

We have become His poetry, a re-created people
that will fulfill the destiny He has given each of us,
for we are joined to Jesus, the Anointed One.
Ephesians 2:10, The Passion Translation

<u>Prompt:</u> Since God is Creator, He has created us to be creative. Keep in mind that you are a unique being, designed to reflect Your Maker's creativity.

How is your life a manifestation of creativity? Be it in your living space, your work place, in a zillion crafts/arts, in everything you do?

For example, my husband Christopher is always coming up with witty fix-it/make-it-up solutions to household/kitchen challenges/problems. Recall some ingenious ways you've solved problems or created remedies.

12

FIRST IMPRESSION

I have heard it said that you can't always trust first impressions, and I would have to agree with that saying. As I look back over the years of my failed human relationships, I see that my first impressions of people have often turned out to be faulty. I had initial illusions about this person or that. Then, after the relationship didn't work out, I became disillusioned.

On the other hand, I have found One Person who remains constant, a true friend. I have come to discover that what He has promised will come to pass, even when I don't see it according to my time schedule. In 1984, I had sensed the Lord was transforming me to be a "safe person", a refuge for people to seek out in the midst of their troubles and struggles. In 1986, God asked me if I would give up everything I owned to follow Him. My two years of this love relationship with Jesus prompted my heart to an excited "Yes." I imagined that my obedience would quickly open the door to the "refuge" vision that I had had two years earlier.

The year 1986 came and went. Had God forgotten the vision He had given me? "I'm ready, Lord!" Two more years; it was October 1989 when I was asked to interview for the Massachusetts halfway house. I almost turned down the opportunity, as it didn't seem to fit my vision. Then I realized that this opportunity was the Lord's way of fulfilling the promise and vision He had given me five years earlier. He was calling me to be a refuge to this houseful of rough, rebellious, hurting men. So, I moved out of state to take my place in the halfway home. And in the transition, I no longer owned my New Jersey life. His vision for me did not come exactly in the time or way or place that I had originally imagined. In God's time, He was exactly on time and on track. The first impression He had given me proved to be trust-worthy.

...the vision is yet for an appointed time,
but at the end, it shall speak, and not lie;
though it tarry, wait for it; it will surely come.
Habakkuk 2:2-3 NKJV

Let's surf over again to www.safeharborministry.org to see some interactive opportunities. And as always, you may find some reasons to shout about your life.

13

SECOND IMPRESSIONS FIND ME REPENTING

Through the years, I have mistakenly judged the messenger; and so, I have not focused on discerning the message. My eye has naturally been drawn to what a person is wearing, particularly when that person is speaking from the pulpit. I have reasoned that the messenger looks gaudy, or perhaps disheveled. The message should be carefully weighed or even disregarded. On the other hand, I have mistaken another messenger's fine appearance and manner as a silent testimony to the message's validity. Wrong! I wonder what my first impression of the carpenter Jesus would have been. I can only hope that my second impression of Jesus would have found me repenting: "Pardon me, Lord. Forgive me!"

As a messenger myself, I have had to struggle with my first impression of the individual or audience before me. Although I may have a message from the Lord to deliver, my subjective read of their faces often throws me. I tell myself that they will never receive the message or that I feel their opposition. However, the Lord, in His mercy, pushes me to open my mouth. Afterwards, I know that the message was right on; that someone needed to hear it. "Thank You, Lord, for giving me a second chance to walk out of my first, fearful impressions. First of all, I am learning to pay attention to Your message given through others to me; and secondly, I am releasing Your message, given through me for others to hear."

God plays no favorites!
It makes no difference who you are or where you are from.
Acts 10:34, The Message

<u>Prompt:</u> How does Scripture reassure you of God's second and third and fourth chances to reassess someone whom you've misjudged?

When have you had to "be yourself", at the risk of being rejected or criticized?

Do you go to God before you attempt to communicate something confrontational or delicate or just plain difficult?

What possible comfort for such "thorny" occasions do you find in the Scriptures?

14

LITTLE MS. CONTROL IS NO LONGER IN CONTROL

From my earliest years, I was a victim of incest. My bedtimes were not a time of rest and peace. Violated and vulnerable, how did I maintain my guard? By fitful wakening. I went off to kindergarten with no conscious awareness of the abuse. But, I was unconsciously acquiring some coping behaviors.

Now, some people are really neat and organized, but this little school-girl learned to create an inordinately orderly bedroom that served as a protective barrier. After all, if I could order my dresses and shoes just so, then I would have a measure of control over my life. So, I proceeded to put everything in order — from the contents of my pencil box to all the books on my shelves. At sixteen, I left my bedroom and my home. Order turned to twenty years of upheaval and chaos. I began to acquire underhanded means to control my life. I learned how to manipulate men to get what I wanted — something to eat, to wear, a place to stay. Eventually, money for my rent, use of their cars, or just a night of dinner, drinks, and drugs with a married man — all the while fiercely guarding my heart. In fact, I purposefully dated men who were safe. They were married and therefore, unavailable. Or they were single deadbeats. I simply used them. I didn't realize I was "courting" dogs because I had no self-worth. I became a pathological scavenger. The price for getting things my way in these controlling relationships – guilt and continual disappointment. Only when I met Jesus as Lord did I begin to relinquish my efforts at controlling my life and men.

Early on in my walk with God, I had a dream. I was driving down a pot-holed highway, and I had no steering wheel. The car was steering perfectly, and I, the driver, was clearly not in control. I never hit one of those potholes. Then, the Lord spoke in the dream, "I AM in control." When I awoke, I smiled at myself: "I do enjoy that five-speed stick shift in my car, but I am willing to let You steer me through life".

Ever since that dream, I have been learning to surrender every steering decision in my life to the Lord. I am learning to enjoy this surrender as a new freedom. I am on the ride of my life! These days, I am living in a beautiful, orderly home (with a reasonably neat husband), and I don't need to or want to control Christopher.

Trust in the LORD with all your heart;
do not depend on your own understanding.
Seek His will in all you do, and He will direct your paths.
Proverbs 3:5-6, NLT

<u>Prompt</u>: This Scripture highlights the ultimate challenge of our human plight – walking in faith!

Are you aware of your trust factor in doing life? On a scale of 1-10, how are you living the faith walk?

There may be areas of faith where you're excelling (in the 8-10 range); other areas of doubt/unbelief where you're flagging in the 1-3 range. Detail those.

Ask Holy Spirit, your Counselor, to illuminate and navigate you through those weak areas.

FREEDOM

To me, an African-American, the word *freedom* has a special ring to it. Some calendars still commemorate Freedom Day on February 1 in memory of that day in 1865, when Abraham Lincoln signed a resolution proposing an amendment to the Constitution to outlaw slavery. Although racism and bigotry still reign in some people's hearts, the constitutional amendment has legally provided for freedom.

Christ, in an even greater measure, has provided for all of mankind's freedom — freedom from sin, death, and eternal slavery to Satan. His freedom loosened me from the slavery of my old lifestyle. Of course, as a born-again believer, my desires are totally different from the old days. I don't want to drink and do drugs anymore. I have no desire to be with other men. I am not interested in the nightlife, the street life, the fast lane. I am free to enjoy the simplicity of a quiet home life, sensible eating, and the companionship of my own husband. I relish my life. I am free to praise the Lord in song and dance throughout the day.

On the other hand, the freedom that Christ brings me does not free me to do whatever I want to do. I am now bound to live according to the Way that Christ and His Holy Spirit choose for me. By the power of His indwelling Spirit, I am able to conform my life to what He sees as best for me. All the guidelines that I need for stress-free, liberated living I can find in the Bible. And His Spirit abides within me to counsel me every step of the way. I am free to walk in love toward others, to live as Jesus would live. I am experiencing this freedom step by step.

So, when an impatient driver is tailgating us and we're going the speed limit or a little above, I am learning to vent, and then pray and bless that driver, "Back off! Help me, Lord. Forgive me, Lord. Bless that driver." And then I continue on with life, forgiving myself, looking for the next opportunity to exercise my new freedom in Christ!

Christ has set us free to live a free life...
Never again let anyone (or anything)
put a harness of slavery on you.
Galatians 5:1 The Message

Prompt: Consider the state of your life. Are you enslaved to any destructive behavior or negative mindset?

Have you taken Jesus to be your Savior? If so, you may still be struggling with life issues. That is not terribly unusual. In the book of Romans (chapter 12, verses 1-2) you'll find a general prescription for dealing with those struggles. Also Galatians 2:20 holds a key, which has to be exercised every day of your life in order to achieve freedom.

If, on the other hand, you're still not decided about accepting Jesus as your Savior, consider asking God about what He'd have you do to resolve this life issue!

It is important to insert here a very important caution. If your emotions and thought life are out of balance, due to a biochemical or hormone imbalance or some other physical abnormality, or substance issue, you may want to seek some kind of intervention from a health practitioner, counselor, spiritual leader, or trusted wise person.

16

PROTECTION

★ ★ ★

Lord, You have reminded me over and over again that even before You saved me, You were protecting me. The lifestyle that I lived should have killed me! One night, I parked my car right in the middle of the street. The next morning, I stumbled out of the front door to get some wake-me-ups (cocaine, black beauties, whatever). My car was gone and I panicked. I glanced up the street, and there was my red-and-black Malibu, smack-dab in the middle of Pearl Place. I didn't even remember driving home, so some angel must have helped me get there. As for the parking, I'll take the blame for that. Angels know how and where to park!

Nobody can tell me that God only sends His angels to protect "real Christians." Some humongous angels must have showed up to protect this prostitute on yet another fateful night. I was trying to get into the apartment of one of my johns when a crazed man came out of the dark. He put a knife in my face, and he wanted one thing — me. I had given myself to all kinds of men for all kinds of reasons (money, drugs, care, and token acceptance), but this violent come-on had me paralyzed with fear. My choice: either let him rape me or end up with a slit throat. Out of nowhere, a passing couple came up behind him. I silently mouthed "rape" to them, and they quietly vanished. My attacker had not seen them and they must have immediately called 911. In minutes, the police showed up — a miracle for that part of the city, which even the police usually avoided. Those "angels," dressed in blue, drew their weapons and killed my fleeing assailant. I would never wish such a violent end for anyone, but who am I to argue with God's protection plan for frightened, mixed-up, lost me?

God saw me in the midst of my perverse lifestyle and protected me anyway. He knew that one day I would leap into His arms, and so He was keeping me safe until then. What a protection plan! When I didn't deserve His mercy, He spared me. How much more now that I am His child can I count on Him to keep and protect me?

Call Me and I'll answer; [I'll] be at your side in bad times.
Psalm 91:15, The Message

Prompt:Do you remember divine rescues in your own life? Had it not been for some unexplainable reason, you might have been involved in a life-ending illness or accident?

Can you imagine the Lord as your lifeguard? Big and small, begin chronicling His rescues in your life.

Think about how many ways you have "rescued" others? From small, practical acts of kindness to actual life-saving interventions; with people you know and with others who just happened into your life. Ponder this and you'll be surprised at what you may recall from your life story.

GRACE

★ ★ ★

Each year I celebrate my spiritual birthday. I have been born again of God since February 15, 1984. I sit here in our home, knowing that it is truly by His grace that I am continuing to walk out my salvation. I know I had no part in earning my salvation. For me, being saved is a gift. "Dear Lord, You reached down and rescued me. I was a wretch like the song says."

Amazing grace, how sweet the sound
That saved a wretch like me
I once was lost, but now I'm found
Was blind, but now I see.[3]

This song was penned by the former captain of a slave ship, John Newton. I share with Newton in proclaiming "now I see." I used to be a slave to sin and evil. Then the Lord got ahold of me, opened my eyes, changed my heart, and set me free. Amazing grace! Even more amazing is that He continues to set me free. He keeps giving me His grace-filled truth about myself. I have journeyed through these years, guided by the truth about God, this life, and eternity's promise. That is His grace at work in me, which continues to amaze me.

"Dear God, thank you for this precious journey that You started me on those many years ago. I am still on my way because of Your grace. It is really Your Way that I am on — which makes it all the more amazing!"

Because of the sacrifice of the Messiah [Jesus Christ], His blood poured out on the altar of the Cross, we're a free people — free of penalties and punishments chalked up by all our misdeeds.

And not just barely free, either. Abundantly free!

He thought of everything, provided for everything we could possibly need, letting us in on the plans He took such delight in making.

*It's in Christ that we find out
who we are and what we are living for.
Long before we first heard of Christ and got our hopes up,
He had His eye on us, had designs on us
for glorious living* [through His grace].
Ephesians 1: 7-9; 11, The Message

<u>Prompt</u>:This Message paraphrased version of Ephesians 1:7-9; 11 is a free-wheeling proclamation of our Christ-bought freedom. It should serve as an absolute go-to on your journey to increasing freedom.

How are you responding in your spirit with this freedom declaration?

What steps do you need to take in your thought life to cooperate with the gift of Jesus' grace?

Refer to Romans 12:1-2 for a divine prescription on how to align your life with His freedom purposes.

How does grace make all of this "do-able"?

46

YOU HAVE BEEN MY RESTORER

At ten years of age, I lived in a world of my own. Hiding from the reality of a lost innocence and suffering from a lack of parental affection, I tried to lose myself in reading. I entered my teens as a problem-waiting-to-happen. In a desperate search for all that I had not found at home, I ran away.

Living the street life did not add up to what I had hoped for. I was looking for love and acceptance, but I never found them. I did find twenty years of alcohol, drugs, and promiscuity, all of which could have killed me. But AIDS and cirrhosis of the liver passed me by. I was still hopeless. I attempted suicide and failed. Nothing could take me out of here.

In 1984, Jesus took me out. Suddenly, I didn't need my addictions or men to provide counterfeit love and acceptance. Why this miraculous and sudden deliverance? As I grew in my knowledge of Christ, I came to know Him as my Restorer. Over these many years, He has healed my emotional wounds and scars of my past. No one heals like the Creator-Doctor!

I remember the day I found a black doll in an antique shop. I purchased her because she is a symbol of the restoration in my life. I named her Amy and have since learned that Amy means beloved or friend (from the French words, *aimer* and *ami*). In Amy, I have a picture of my lost childhood being restored to me. And unlike the dolls of my childhood, Amy is a little "chocolate doll," just like me.

If you are feeling a loss or experiencing devastation from your past, why not entrust yourself to the Restorer, to the Healer? Just as He has restored me, He can restore you. No pain or loss is impossible for Him to heal.

He restores my soul.
Psalm 23:5, NKJV

<u>Prompt:</u> Have you ever experienced the Lord as Restorer?

Do you know Him as the Lover of your soul?

See **Soul Keeping**, John Ortberg (Zondervan, Grand Rapids, MI). Also, check out Dallas Willard's writings. Willard's longtime mentoring of Ortberg profoundly shaped his writing of **Soul Keeping**.

19

SELF-DEATH

The English prophet Graham Cooke says that there are two beings out to kill us — God and Satan. Well, I'd rather have God kill me any day! So, every day I have thousands of occasions (mostly in my thought life) where I can choose to die to self-centered desires, self-generated plans, self-righteous criticism and judging, and selfish ambition. These are all opportunities to live a God-centered, God-generated life - free of judgements and ambition. Navigating this process of dying to self is about choices. In putting this Scriptural principle of self-death into practice, we must rely on the Holy Spirit's nudging, prompting, and empowering. Christian teacher and author, Joyce Meyer, observes that the process of dying to self is worked out in *the battlefield of the mind* [and its corresponding emotions][4]. No human is spared from this battle; not even Jesus was exempt. His three "face-off confrontations" with Satan's temptations were fought in the forty days of wilderness. That wilderness battle in Jesus' mind, will, and decisions was all about dying to self. Jesus' resisting the plots of Satan culminated in the Garden of Gethsemane and on the Hill of the Skull (Calvary). His crucifixion, the mysterious, ultimate act of selflessness, made way for all humanity to be redeemed from self, sin (and death, the grave and hell).

While I have never had to face the agony of a Gethsemane or death on a cross, I do remember an agonizing season of struggle in the summer of 2018, where I had to choose between my plans and aspirations, plus my six-month-long standing commitment to a leadership role in an upcoming conference <u>versus</u> God's slowly emerging, preferred plan for me. Would I choose to fulfill a leader's expectation of me, which would vault me into a con-spicuous limelight of conference leadership? Or would I obey Holy Spirit's contradictory hinting and whispering? And I say hinting and whispering because the voices surrounding me (including my husband's and my spiritual dad's) were encouraging me, even prodding me to fulfill my long-standing commitment. With only two months remaining until the conference, my days and nights became restless. I was wrestling with the ever-growing conviction that I could not go ahead with those human, self-generated con-ference plans. But still I had not told the conference host. Then my restlessness developed into a body manifestation. The numbness I was feeling in my left shoulder and arm, I rebuked in Jesus's name. "Devil, you will not hold me back from my ministry." And then on my way to another leadership assignment, six weeks before my planned conference "debut," I felt a stabbing pain radiate through my shoulders and arm. I had gone into the meeting place early, but then had to rush back to the car where I collapsed on the pas-senger seat. Christopher drove me home. Ten days of pain and sleeplessness followed. On that tenth day, the conference team met to finalize everything for the big event. Right in the middle of our session, I could scarcely sit. Writhing in spasms, I jumped up and heading for the front door, I gasped out, "I can't do this!" The next day, I announced my decision to the conference host, "I must step away; I can't do this conference."

Looking back on those days, I now see that my dramatic obedi-ence flew in the face of everyone's expectations. But I knew God was requiring this death-to-self decision. And you know what? Within two days, the throbbing spasms ceased and I made a two-hundred-mile round-trip sitting comfortably next to my driving husband. In my mind, I have always known that on the other side of death is resurrection, and that is a good thing. The process of dying to self does not feel good, but I desire to trust God in assisting me to die to me. I have a choice: to abandon myself to the process or to hold onto my way. My way will surely lead to a dead end (and maybe another left shoulder and arm season, or worse). Lord forbid! When the Spirit is prompting me how to move, speak, even think, I don't want to be slow to hear and obey. Spare me from the I/me/mine life!

I have been crucified with Christ. My ego is no longer central.
It is no longer important that I appear righteous...
Christ lives in me. The life you see me living is not mine,
but is lived by the faith [or really, **lived by the faithfulness**]
of the Son of God who loved me and gave himself for me.
Galatians 2:20 The Message

We aren't leaving you hanging without an interactive opportunity! Go to www.safeharborministry.org.

OBEDIENCE

Five years into the Jesus life brought me to a turning point that I could never have imagined. Most of those five years, I had been shadowing my mentor, former prison chaplain Leroy Holmes. After accompanying Pastor Holmes into several prisons and jails, he invited me to a summit meeting of COPE (Coalition of Prison Evangelists). Pastor Holmes introduced me to his colleague, Rev. James Spence from Massachusetts. "Pastor Holmes tells me that you could very well be the person we need for our halfway house in Massachusetts. You'd be counselling parolees in a residential, faith-based program at the Bridge House outside of Boston. Could you send us your resume?" I was caught off-guard, but responded "Sure." Later, I questioned my mentor, "What is going on here?" He grinned, "We had a board meeting this morning and I brought up your name. Jim told us he needed a good man to replace a counselor he'd just fired. I told him I had the perfect candidate, 'But Jim, she's not a man.' So, bottom line, when God opens a door, you just walk through it. Sister Sharon, just send your resume." Well, I reluctantly sent off a resume; a week later, I got a call from the Bridge House. Would I be available to come to Massachusetts for an interview? Caught off-guard again, I said "Yes." Reverend Spence was delighted, "Good, we'll set up a time for next week. I'll call you back with the details."

Several hours later, a knock at my door, "It's Pastor Holmes." Now his grin was sheepish, "And you have some news?" I wanted to respond, "Get out of here." Instead, I listened as he reminded me, "When God opens a door, you definitely want to walk through it." I countered, "But I don't have any money to go." Pastor Holmes' quick retort "Well, you know what, we'll have a benefit service and raise enough money to send you to Massachusetts." *I don't want to go to no Massachusetts.* He must have been heard my street-talk, push-back thought! "Better yet, Sister Sharon, I have a tin of saved money in the church van. Let me go downstairs and I will get it."

The next thing I knew, I was on a bus to the New York Port Authority; then a Peter Pan coach to Newton, Massachusetts. Reader, you've already read about my meeting and interviewing with Rev. Spence. My accepting the counselor's position and moving to Massachusetts proved to be that pivotal decision that would change the entire course of my life. But to arrive at that turning point involved a series of decisions to surrender and obey the promptings of the Spirit (and the prodding of Pastor Holmes, my Spirit-led, on-the-ground coach).

When I moved to Massachusetts two months later, there followed weeks and months of wanting to pack up and go back to New Jersey. I called my coach and he reminded me, "Every step of the way to your assignment at the Bridge House has been because of your obeying God's promptings." My protest, "But you don't under-stand. My own family has disapproved of my move. I've been told that there's talk around town that I've been irresponsible for going off and leaving my family." My obedience to leave and go had cost me my family's disapproval, my reputation. And now I was feeling the pain of separation from my church family and Pastor Holmes. I didn't need to look for any other reasons to flee Massachusetts. But in the process of feeling the pain and experiencing the con-flicting tugs, I ended up yielding to God. Rather than trying to please my hometown critics and to ease my mis-informed guilty conscience, I gained a huge victory by obeying God's promptings and Pastor Holmes' stern reprimand.

No one, not even I, understood that I was on a mission. "I'm willing to continue to obey You. Help me, help me, help me, Lord." In the grander scheme of my life-trek, the pain brought great gain.

Is there some pending decision in your life that may entail pain but demands obedience? Remember, sometimes pain leads to godly gain. (One big gain awaited me in Massachusetts; my husband-to-be, Christopher, lived in Massachusetts.)

In the wounds of a friend [Pastor Holmes' admonitions proved to be a wounding, straight out of Proverbs 27:6!]
... listen to Him! Plain listening is the thing ...
1st Samuel 15:22, The Message

<u>Prompt</u>:Think of painful decisions you've faced. How have you experienced victory in doing the right thing?

Are there any instances of disobedience that resulted in greater pain?

What "obedience/pain/gain lessons" have you learned over the years?

How about reprimands either from God (or from others) that have been valuable? Life changing?

MERCY

★ ★ ★

Years ago, I came to know a strong faith-woman whom we'll call Brenda. We became close, talking on the phone nearly every day, and visiting at each other's homes. We were peers; someone I could talk to, someone who understood the challenges of being a counselor and a ministry leader. But, in the course of time, communications became strained. We saw less and less of each other. She had stopped calling. So, because I tend to express myself, my feelings, and my thoughts without holding back, I wanted to get this whole impasse out in the open. I called several times. No answer. I left voicemails. I even wrote her a letter. No response. I felt hurt, angry, and, then, vindictive. In fact, I wanted to drop by her apartment and tell her off (and, who knows, maybe slap her). On another occasion, I wanted my husband to stop by her place and confront her. In the midst of all these imaginations, the Lord's Word popped up on my imaginary screen: "What does the Lord require of you but to love mercy" (Micah 6:8). Hmm… hadn't I preached that Scripture to a large, ecumenical gathering of pastors, ministers, and leaders back in the early 1990s? And several years later, there it was – right in my face. Uhh-oh! Amazing!

Amazing how the Spirit was now cautioning me with my own preaching words. A divine intervention of mercy. As I listened up, I recall hearing Him say, "You must not react, but rather respond as if nothing had been done to you." That months-long drama of living in conflict with Brenda began to dissipate. I thought of Jesus, for example, who experienced betrayal from His friend Judas. Jesus did not strike back or pay back. So, why should I?

As I look back over my thirty-some years of Jesus-living, I'm amazed at the endless mercies I've received. I'm so mindful of His mercy that I'll need to continue living the God-life. Even now I have just come through a new challenge in yet another relationship with ... you guessed it, a peer! This time, a male leader whom we'll call Chad; we've talked and processed our differences, our offenses. And there is a certain resolution. "I need your wisdom, your healing, and, most of all, your mercy, Lord." I know God's mercy has been working on my willingness to forgive others. He has opened my heart to my Healer. Step by step, I have extended forgiveness and mercy to Chad without him even knowing about it. The Lord has worked His miraculous way in my heart, over and over again. Oh, how I love His mercy, and how much more am I ready to extend mercy.

What do You require of me but mercy?
Micah 6:8, personal paraphrase

Prompt:How have people shown you mercy? How might those situations have gone had mercy not been granted?

What does the Bible have to say about the Lord's mercies? Strong's Exhaustive Concordance of the Bible pinpoints the word *mercy* or *mercies* in several hundred verses!

FORGIVENESS

Forgive <u>all</u> the people who have wronged me? I never thought I could. Forgive the family member who sexually abused me? Forgive the white people who were rude to me, a skinny African-American teenager waitressing at the local Howard Johnson's in the 1960s? Forgive the cosmetology teacher who referred to me and my friend as "you people"? Forgive everyone who objected to me being engaged to Christopher (a white man)?

Forgiveness is a challenging command straight from the Master Himself. "If you don't forgive those who offend, who abuse you, who mistreat you, how can you expect Your Heavenly Father to forgive you all of your offenses?" (Mark 11:26). I've screamed, "Ohhhhhhh-nooo. I can't. I won't. I don't know how. And I don't want to know how." But in the end, I had to start the process. I have crawled and gagged my way to forgive those who have trespassed against me. It's God who has led me through the painful process of extending forgiveness toward those trespassers. At times, I actually refused to cooperate. In the end, He won, as I surrendered to His command. Nevertheless, we all have to heed His command to forgive.

I officiated at the funeral of the family member who sexually abused me as a child. The title of the funeral message I preached? "Forgiveness"! I think the Holy Spirit held my hand (and my tongue) all the way through the message. I never even hinted at my abuse nor at my forgiveness issue with the deceased. The fact that I harbored no bitterness had cleared the way for me to bring the message of forgiveness as a life application for everyone at the funeral.

I came away from the funeral with a greater belief in the power of forgiveness. You too, friend, can begin to forgive today, right now. In your mind and with your mouth and with the Spirit by your side, try saying, "I forgive you, (*pronounce that person's name*)." Memories may flood in with a "NO WAY." You'll probably experience a battle between declaring forgiveness (which is a faith step) and feelings (which are the emotional fallout of the traumatic event and memories). Be willing to have God walk you through the process of forgiving that unforgivable person. I'm not saying that it is going to be an easy process; I would never tell you to "get over it." The Awesome Forgiver will meet you in the midst of your hurt, your anger, your rage, and your devastation. Only be willing to begin the process. **Note of caution**: Any serious trauma may require therapy and wise counsel. In other words, don't try the process of extending forgiveness on your own if you have been experiencing major emotional upheaval or radical mood changes in your day-to-day living.

If you have anything against someone,
forgive; only then will [God] wipe your slate clean.
Mark 11:26, The Message

Prompt:In your journal, which should be kept safe and secure, away from anyone else's eyes, start to list those hurts, offenses, abuses, slights, and insults that may be replaying in your memory.

Begin the forgiveness process; maybe you should start with a mild offense first. For example, your second grade teacher who wouldn't choose you for the class play. Just say, "_____, I forgive you. I know you didn't mean me any harm."

It is possible to address major offenses on your own, depending on the overall health of your soul and your emotional stability. **But please, if you do not feel up to doing this process by yourself,** feel free to speak with a reputable spiritual leader, counselor, or therapist. Particularly, if the offence caused you trauma, physical or emotional. Verbal abuse can inflict deep soul wounding. Ask a trusted friend to recommend someone who is qualified to treat your trauma. **Do not** consult "alternative" healers, psychics, or "new age" mediums.

INTIMACY

Intimacy, as portrayed in the Bible, is a deep relationship of knowing each other. Husband and wife, in the book of Genesis, were created to know each other in conjugal intimacy. In the same way, Joseph knew Mary after she gave birth to Jesus.

But in a mysterious, deeper way, God created humanity, His creation of man and woman, for intimate fellowship with Himself. Adam and Eve enjoyed daily fellowship with their Creator in the Garden of Eden. But when Adam and Eve strayed into fellowship with the Deceiver (Satan), they lost that intimacy with their Creator. Although we can't be in the garden to find that original intimacy with God, we can regain a measure of that Garden-of-Eden intimacy.

The early part of each day is my best time to come away to be alone with God. In the midst of our busy, modern lives, our challenge is to make intimacy with God a top priority. This has become an increasingly vital part of my day. In fact, I have found that my day doesn't go very well if I skip that daily intimacy with God. I remember first reading *The Secret Place*, an exhortation to pursue intimacy with the Lord. Author Dr. Dale A. Fife points to "the hiding place" or "the secret place." At my first waking moment, I find my secret place by talking with the Lord. I am pursuing intimacy with my heavenly Father, my elder brother Jesus, and my sweet Holy Spirit! I have to do this— for me and for everyone my life touches.

Ask God to give you the desire to pursue intimacy with Him. It may be a deeper place you crave. Or, maybe there's your relentlessness that will find you pushing all distractions aside. Being close to my Maker and Lover is my lifeline for my very existence and well-being. If we're honest with ourselves, we know deep down inside that nothing or no one else will do. In fact, we'll end up being miserable and irritable if we neglect pursuing that special, secret place which He has prepared for us. That place may be in the bathroom or the bedroom or the kitchen or sitting in your car. Seek it. Seek Him! If you are too busy, then you probably are! May you find a way to create a time and place to know Him personally, intimately! Someone reading this right now may not be able to spend much time upon waking. Just so you know, intimacy can be found anywhere, any time. Maybe it's a chunk of time before laying your head on your pillow, whatever the time of day or night. Your life depends on it. And all through your waking hours, you'll find it easier to "place" the Lord in all your comings, your goings, and your doings.

I gave up all that inferior stuff so I could know Christ personally.
Philippians 3:10, The Message

<u>Prompt</u>: Our companion verse here in Chapter 23 ("*I gave up all that inferior stuff…*") may serve as a prompt for you to inventory your "inferior stuff." Get out your journal; start jotting that stuff down. Have fun; be real; even laugh at yourself. It's okay.

Seriously though, it's healthy to confess your stuff to your journal and to your Creator; to your spouse; to a trusted person, someone of your own gender. Be careful to talk things over with a genuine confidant – someone who will listen and keep it confidential. No one can "fix" you. But there may be that special person who will be your venting person; someone to whom you can "let it all out." It's so liberating to unlock yourself to God and to a fellow being.

Coming clean with God is a beautiful thing. Having a brother closer than any other, a sister closer than any other, is a beautiful thing.

SUFFERING

★ ★ ★

It seems that suffering has been my constant companion. I don't mean to say that I have suffered the horrors of war or persecution, but I have suffered the more subtle pain of emotional trauma and emotional deprivation. Childhood sexual abuse is a horror; it has left me feeling violated. My parents' unaffectionate ways left me feeling isolated. So, from an early age, I perceived myself as unloved and unlovable. Adulthood found me bandaging my pain with alcohol, drugs, and men. The scars on my wrists remind me how desperately I wanted to lose my life.

When I came to know Christ in 1984, I began to experience a reversal of the emotional suffering. I have received much inner healing. I have been able to process my childhood abuse and childhood emotional deprivation. But I am quick to remind myself that even as a deeply committed Christian, I will experience some pain and suffering as long as I am in this world. Relationships with people will not always work out. Church life will fall short of my expectations. I will even get disillusioned with myself.

Comparing my life now — and its relatively small sufferings — with the enormity of my pain before I came to know the Lord, I have to stop and be grateful. In his first letter, the apostle Peter addresses the persecuted Christ-followers of the first-century Roman Empire. His advice is a proper perspective on suffering [see the referenced Scriptures below]. He reminds us that suffering (and this life on earth) are short-lived compared to experiencing heaven for eternity. Alcohol, drugs, and suicide attempts are things of my past. I struggle through the lesser sufferings of today, like rejection from family or former friends. I may cry or get despondent or angry (and I do all of these occasionally). My heart's desire is that I remember to follow the words of Peter.

You're not the only ones plunged into...hard times.
It's the same with Christians all over the world.
So, keep a firm grip on faith. The suffering won't last forever.

It won't be long before this generous God who has great plans
for us in Christ — eternal and glorious plans they are! —
will have you put together and on your feet for good.
He gets the last word; yes, he does!
1st Peter 5:10, The Message

<u>Prompt</u>: What is your current experience of suffering or pain?

Another way of exploring this suffering dilemma is to ask the Spirit, "What do I have to put up, keeping a firm grip on faith, empowered by Your Spirit?" Take a look at Galatians 5:22-23 where longsuffering is depicted as a fruit of the Spirit. In other words, "I can't do this without Your Spirit, Lord".

Paul puts it this way in Romans 8:28: "All these things [suffering and pain] are working for the good of those who love Him, who are called according to His purpose." Think out loud with your pen or keypad. How does this Romans' passage apply to my life?

COMFORT

I will never forget Memorial Day weekend 1994. As I hobbled out of the Florida National Guard Armory auditorium, my lower back and legs throbbed with pain. Christopher had to carry my handbag and my Jacksonville Theological Seminary diploma, as he helped me across the parking lot. Just then, fellow graduate Dave drove up alongside us. "Hang in there, sister, because you will experience His comfort in the midst of this discomfort. And then down the road, you'll be able to comfort others who are hurting." That wasn't exactly what I wanted to hear right then. How about a parking lot miracle healing, or at least, something to make the pain go away?

The next morning, as I attempted to get out of our motel bed, I collapsed on the floor. "Honey, I can't get up." Christopher had to drag me to the bathroom. I was virtually immobile from the waist down. In those days with a stubborn faith and no insurance, I was determined to await a healing. I spent days writhing in pain, flat on my back in that Jacksonville Holiday Inn, wondering if I would ever walk again. What was that parking lot word from Dave? Comfort? Well, right there in my crisis, I was able to comfort a young woman who was staying two doors down the hall from us. My husband had encountered her in the lobby and sensed that she was troubled. Christopher told her to call our room. She called, and I invited her over. She poured out her heart, sharing her wayward lifestyle. Receiving Jesus' forgiveness, she left our room, resolved to end a relationship with her abusive partner down the hall from us. There I was passing out comfort while waiting for my own comfort.

Very soon after that, my comfort began to manifest in the person of Dr. Harold Vick, Sr., president of the seminary, who had heard of my plight. Showing up at our room, he arranged for my ambulance transport to his trusted chiropractor. An X-ray, a finessed adjustment, and my reversed neck-spine curvature reverted to almost normal – all within an hour. Three weeks of chiropractic therapy followed before I would be able to safely take the three-day car trip home to Massachusetts. Before the chiropractor would release me to travel, he made Christopher promise to stop driving every couple of hours so I could get out and walk as part of my recovery therapy.

Comfort upon comfort. From day one of my treatment, this wonderful chiropractor had declared, "You are missionaries, Sharon and Christopher. I will take care of you at no cost until you are able to drive back to Massachusetts." And Dr. Vick paid for our ten days at the Holiday Inn. And guess who called us on the tenth day? Dave. "Hey, I heard from Dr. Vick what's going on with y'all. Wanta' come out and stay with us till you ready to go back north? Me and Kim got a double-wide – way outta' town." For the next ten days before heading back north, we stayed in their double-wide mobile home guest room. And while we were there, we comforted Kim with her pile of baby clothes and diapers. We bought them a nice secondhand washing machine. I thought, *Dave, I remember your words in the parking lot. You declared that I would comfort others, even as I have been comforted.*

He comes alongside us when we go through hard times,
and before you know it, He brings us alongside someone else
who is going through hard times so that we can be there
for that person just as God was there for us
2nd Corinthians 1:3-4, The Message

<u>Prompt</u>:Does this biblical concept of comfort-receiving, comfort-sharing resonate with your life experience?

Have you found it to work in your own life?

What about other people you know or know of where this comfort principle actually has worked?

26

ROCK IN MY LIFE

★ ★ ★

Every Labor Day weekend, as a little girl, I went with my family to the beach in Wildwood, New Jersey. This was a perfect way to end the summer. My favorite pastime there was collecting rocks and pebbles by the seashore. Hours would go by while I hunted for different shapes and colors, all the time fascinated with their variety.

Thirty years later, I came to a saving knowledge of the Lord. In my work and ministry, I began to travel up and down the East Coast. Everywhere I went, I began to pick up local rocks. I married and now my husband joins me in bringing rocks home from wherever — the Hometown Buffet parking lot in Delaware; from Waterhouse, Jamaica; Mwanza in Tanzania, East Africa. These large and small rocks, laid out all around our home — in corners, on windowsills and tables, in baskets and in glass vases — remind me of the hymn "Rock of Ages".

In the Bible, many references portray the Lord as a rock. King David, in the book of Psalms, said, "Lead me to the Rock that is higher than I" (Psalm 61:2). Second Samuel 22:32 asks, "Who is a rock, except our God?" According to Deuteronomy 32:18, "He is the Rock who gave you life."

All through my life, even before I came to Him, He was there, solid and unmovable, keeping me safe in the midst of trauma, danger, and my fool-heartedness. He is my Rock-Foundation, my Fortress-Rock, and my Rock of Strength.

*The Lord lives! Blessed be my **Rock**!*
*Let God be exalted, the **Rock** of my salvation!*
2nd Samuel 22:47, NKJV

<u>Prompt</u>: Meditate on the following quote (source unknown; I don't remember where I encountered it.): "Think of the Lord as your Mighty Rock. You can stand firm on Him. Let Him stabilize your heart and mind, your emotions and thoughts with His rock-solid Self."[5]

Use that quote to craft a personal prayer: "I will always think of you, Lord, as my Mighty Rock. I can stand firm on You"(and so forth).

Write it out as a declaration; enter in your journal; post it on your wall, on your mirror.

AIN'T GONNA LET NO ROCK

Two thousand years ago on the first Palm Sunday, not everyone in the crowded streets was excited about Jesus entering the city of Jerusalem. Although many people lavished praises on the donkey-riding Messiah, some of the religious leaders protested to Jesus, "'Teacher, get your disciples under control.' Jesus said, 'If they keep quiet, the stones would cry out in praise to Me'" (Lk. 19:39-40).

I decided long ago that I wasn't going to remain silent and have a bunch of stones take my place in praising God. Never that! That doesn't mean that I have to have goose-bump experiences in order to praise God. At times, I have felt stone-cold with doubts and fears. A cloud of isolation may have a hold on me. But, I make up my mind to sing to the Rock of my salvation. My home is a place of praise, prayer, worship. We have a lot of rocks laid out all over our house, but I am the one who gives praises to the living God. No need for the rocks around here to cry out.

In the song *We Need to Hear from You*[6], Steve Fry and his worship team declare with defiant shouts:

Ain't gonna let no rock out-praise me
Ain't gonna let it sing in my place
Jesus is still worthy
To receive our praise
With holy hands uplifted and voices raised
We are shouting and singing
Hosanna; blessed is the King
Though Pharisees [and self] try to quiet our worship
We will shout to the Lord and sing.

I have experienced freedom as I sang to Him. I have felt dark clouds of discouragement lift as I have lifted up praises to Jesus. But in the end, it is not about feeling; it is about being obedient to Jesus. I will praise Him. No rock will have to fill in for me. And when I am really struggling, I'll go into the bathroom, get in the steamy shower, and muster up a song of my own. Before you know it, I am shouting praises to my Rock-King.

If you keep quiet, the stones will do it for you, shouting praise.
Luke 19:40, (paraphrase based on <u>The Message</u>).

<u>Prompt</u>:Do you ever feel unable or unwilling to thank God? Not able to praise God? Or maybe this whole concept of thanking God or praising God is foreign to you?

Opposing emotions of doubt, fear, and feeling isolated tend to stifle gratitude, praise, and worship.

Do you resort to God-focusing in order to deal with negative emotions? Try it; praise Him. Worship Him. Thank Him!

PERSEVERANCE

Perseverance, according to the World Book Dictionary, is "never giving up what one has set out to do."[7] In other words, "to keep going on, to not abandon your goal." Writing and publishing this book has proved to be an ongoing lesson in perseverance. The story behind *Why I Shout* was conceived when my life-direction turned to Jesus in 1984. I gave my life to Christ and began to shout with gratitude. Then, seven years later, I met Christopher. Enjoying our first lunch date together, I heard him say, "You're going to write a book." I shot back, "So, what's the title?" Out of nowhere, he prophesied, *"Why I Shout!"*; a twinkling-vision of actually writing my story in 1984. Perseverance and another thirteen years delivered the first edition of this book. This book was surely God-inspired, but for so long, it just wasn't happening. In fact, the vision had to die, with any hope for publication lying cold and forgotten. Well, Holy Spirit hadn't forgotten. God eventually resurrected the vision and the necessary inspiration.

Twelve years into our marriage, there was a moment of conception: my seed ideas and life experiences; Christopher's word-smithing. What you are reading right now is the final result of a sentence or two here; a paragraph there; at best, a page or so. Weeks would go by with no keyboarding. Finally, thirty-one rough-draft chapters, a smoother second draft, and a third finished draft. The original publication with Pneuma Books in 2004, and now this new generation, the third edition in 2020. Thanks to the publishing team at Xulon Press for their wrap-around finesse, you are looking at the fruit of perseverance.

The lessons learned in all those years of waiting and dying to the vision of a book have found me and my husband marveling at how God worked it all out. God wanted all of me (Sharon) to surrender first of all. He allowed me to be frustrated in my efforts at making the book happen. The book project had become an obsession. At first I cried out in my frustration. I eventually understood that I really needed to be crying out for Him, not the book. I had no option but to give in to Him and the dead book. Then it really sunk in. As I desired more of Him, He brought to pass the desire of my heart — to birth this book. But it all started when I persevered in my relationship with God. I am spending more time pursuing God and allowing my life, like the book, to be an ongoing work brought forth in His way!

I've got my eye on the goal,
where God is beckoning us onward — to Jesus.
Let's keep focused on the goal,
those of us who want everything God has for us.
Philippians 3:14, The Message

Prompt:What do you know of the tension between persevering and surrendering?

Have you experienced in the process of waiting a favorable outcome?

Is there a "waiting and persevering, persevering and waiting" that you are experiencing right now? How has Holy Spirit (your Counselor) been prompting you? Something to conceive, to gestate, to birth, to grow? Is there something needing adjustment or therapy? Or, perhaps, a burial?

YOU SING IT LIKE I LIVE IT, PHIL DRISCOLL

I glanced around at the hushed crowd of Sunday worshippers. There's the cue for my solo worship dance. My knees are quaking as the CD track starts to play. *"Walk with Me, Jesus"* resonates throughout the acoustic expanse of the seaside church. I wish I could feel Jesus right now. I hear the lyrics, "... the road is too rocky to make it alone." *Very rocky*, I think. Then I remember how far I have come. I used to dance in go-go bars during the 1970s and 80s. Now I have a husband, my only dancing partner. Christopher turns the volume up, and I take off. My legs and my knees are all working. My feet glide along the smooth oak floor. Phil Driscoll's throaty voice spurs me on.

Dance with me, Jesus
On this life-journey
The road is too rocky
To make it alone [8]

The memories of my old life flash by. Jesus walked me through the stupor of alcohol and drugs. And here He is, now leading me in dance on a Sunday morning at this affluent church. I twirl to celebrate how the Shepherd has walked me through it all. He protected me, a welfare mother living with an abusive, addicted husband. I survived the race riots of Newark, New Jersey. Here I am dancing in God's house. I am the honored guest, the very first worship dancer (and the only African-American female to ever minister in that church). I break out into long strides of freedom, as I let Jesus propel me through the aisles.

Later, as everyone gathered for refreshments, a tall, matronly woman approached me with congratulations. "My dear, you remind me of Judith Jamison." I politely accepted the compliment. Under my breath, I thanked God that someone had recently made the same kind of remark about my dancing. I had to ask that person, "Who is Judith Jameson?" I learned that she was a famous African-American ballet dancer. I could only smile. You see, I have never had a ballet lesson in my life. But I do know that Holy Spirit is my dance teacher! I'll let Phil Driscoll sing it. And Phil, thanks, because in your singing, you remind me that this is how I live: "Dance with me, Jesus ...the road is too rocky to make it alone."

You will never leave me or forsake me.
Hebrews 13:5, personalized,
based on the <u>New King James Version</u>

Do you ever have the sense that you are actually walking or dancing with Jesus?

Even if you didn't feel it tangibly, think of those times when <u>it had to be</u> Him walking you through!

How could you prepare your soul for knowing Jesus as the One who "will never leave you, never forsake you"? (Hebrews 13:5) [Buy **Soul Keeping**, John Ortberg – a two-book interactive text and study guide; these are wonderful "paradigm-tools" to cultivate your soul for a closer walk with Jesus

I AM BEING PRUNED (OUCH!)

Have you ever felt as if your life is too cluttered or complicated? Confused? Maybe you are simply worn out, too busy. Perhaps you are forever fretting. Or, you are struggling with a sin issue that just won't be shaken?

I have faced all of the above predicaments. I've been at a loss to resolve them. But you and I know who has a solution, an answer, a way for us to deal with our life problems. His Way may not be our way (or our idea of a solution or answer). Take a look at the end-of-chapter Scripture below. The operative words: *prune*, *lop off*, which remind me of my many house-plants and indoor tropical trees. I consider how Jesus, through His love, has pruned me over the years (and is still pruning me). I love my plants, but every now and then I have to cut them back. I always talk to them as I get ready to get out trimming scissors. I say, "This may hurt, babies. However, it will be good for you." That's just how Jesus deals with me; He cuts back some of the stuff in my life if I'll let Him. Like the plant that has been cut back, I too can grow back fuller and healthier than before. Jesus never promises me that the cutting won't hurt, but eventually I do feel better and my life begins to flourish after the pruning.

Jesus is pruning us for our own good (and for His own good purposes). In fact, His desire is to have His children yield to the divine pruning. The New King James translation refers to this cutting back as *purging* and *pruning*. This procedure involves a cleansing or a purifying as well as a trimming, a cutting or a removing. The next time you feel as if something in your life is being removed, think of the Gardener lopping off excess or useless stuff, even sin. It may not feel good, but it is something the Lord wants you to get rid of. So don't automatically blame your discomfort on the devil. You may just need to be pruned; your life will be more fruitful as a result. And if you are anything like me, you will find that Jesus will be back again for more pruning. Why? Because He loves you and wants you to experience a fruitful life for your own good. The truth is that pruning and growth is His way and, ultimately, for my contentment. On the other hand, my way equals "no ouch now," but no fruit later; and most likely a withered life, and eventual PAIN. So, will you let Him prune you?

He lops off every branch that doesn't produce.
And He prunes those branches that bear fruit for even larger crops.
John 15:2, The Living Bible

Prompt:Any thoughts on the pruning He may have in store for you?

It's ok not to know. Try sitting quietly with a journal and some thoughts may come to mind. You may want to start by just asking, "Lord, what do you want to prune?"

What is impossible for you to accomplish on your own is do-able in His strength and by His grace. Take it easy. Look up Matthew 11:28-30 (check out The Message version. Download the app. <Bible +1>). In the New King James Version, Jesus reminds us that He will walk alongside us, bearing our burdens.

31

A NEW NAME

While riding around in the car, my husband and I were listening to "I Will Change Your Name." (I can't remember who did that song; I wish I could give credit to the vocalist and the writer.) That song reminded me of a recent dream in which the Lord appeared to me and actually changed my name. I don't remember the specific name that He bestowed on me. I do know that I had a new name (and therefore, a new identity).

In Scripture, the Lord promises to give a new name to all people of all history who are His. In the book of Revelation, the entire population of heaven lives in the New Jerusalem. So we, His people, are destined to be citizens of the New Jerusalem. Therefore, we will be "New Jerusalemite citizens"; every one of us will have a new, God-given name to complement our identity in God's forever heaven.

In the meantime, while we are still on this earth, we can walk in the prophetic promise given to Isaiah (see the Scriptures below), knowing that our name and identity are being worked out here every day.

You may be wondering what God can do with your life to fulfill that promise to redeem you into someone whole and beautiful. The new name God has for you means that you will no longer be called wounded, outcast, lonely, or afraid; no longer devalued, discounted, dismissed. In your new identity, you will be confident, joyful, faithful, and overcoming. You will be a friend of God who seeks His face! Rejoice and be glad. Remember that the following prophecy from Isaiah applies to you. And remember this whole book points us to what He can do and will do if we'll only let Him. As the old Sunday school chorus goes, "Trust and obey, for there's no other way to be happy in Jesus but to trust and obey."

You'll get a brand-new name straight from the mouth of God.
You'll be a stunning crown in the palm of God's hand;
a jeweled gold cup held high in the hand of your God.

No more will anyone call you Rejected,
You will be called Hephzibah [My Delight].

Because God delights in you ... as a young man
marries his virgin bride, so your builder marries you,
and as a bridegroom is happy with his bride,
so your God is happy with you.
Isaiah 62:2-5, The Message

Prompt:You know what I'm going to suggest, don't you? Get out your journal if it's not already out. Start a free flow of your thoughts and imaginations about you and who you're becoming.

WE ARE AT THE END OF OUR READ BUT...

How would you summarize all that you've been experiencing with *Why I Shout* and your journal? Sum up your overarching reasons for shouting – your major gains of ground in your perspective. For example, you can choose to shout in the surety of His forgiveness toward you; in the hope of His promises for you; in celebration of your overcomings; in the confidence that God will work in you both to will and do what pleases Him. Big picture; final thoughts. But you may want to do another cycle through your journal. Just know we can continue on growing with more of Jesus living through me and in me.

I, Sharon Nzwalla Ryan and my husband, Christopher Capen Ryan, have been tasked by the Shepherd to shepherd Safe Harbor Ministry. We are yoked with the Luke 4:18-19 mandate to bring healing, freeing, and redeeming through the power of Jesus Christ to the hurting, the abused, the hopeless, and the discontent. Also to those who are doing alright but are wanting more … more of God, more buy-in to the gospel, more commitment to His kingdom mission. Do we want to make a difference with our families and our neighbors, to impact our communities, our regions, our nations, the world? All who are willing, listen up:

> **God authorized and commanded Me** [Jesus] **to commission you** [dear readers]: **"Go out and train everyone you meet, far and near, in this way of life, marking them by baptism in the threefold name, Father, Son, and Holy Spirit. Then instruct them in the practice of <u>all</u> I have commanded you. I** [the Great-I-Am, Yahweh, Adonai, Father-God, Abba] **will be with you as you <u>do this</u>, day after day after day, right up to the end of the age."** (Matthew 28:18-20, <u>The Message</u>)

REFERENCES

1. A paraphrase of Philippians 4:13 (any Bible translation)

2. *Do I Trust You?*, Twila Paris (Signature Songs, Brentwood Benson)

3. *Amazing Grace*, John Newton (common domain?)

4. <u>Battlefield of the Mind</u>, Joyce Meyer (Faith Words/1999)

5. No clue where this approximation quote came from! Let us know if you can source it, research-reader.

6. *We Need to Hear From You*, Bethel Praise (K. Singleton & D. Baron), Warner-Alliance

7. World Book Encyclopedia Dictionary, Chicago, IL

8. *Walk With Me Jesus,* <u>I'm A Different Man</u>, Phil Driscoll (J. Douglas & D. Burgess), Word Records

QUANTITY DISCOUNTS ARE AVAILABLE FOR BULK ORDERS.

To book Sharon Nzwalla Ryan for a speaking engagement or media interview.

Contact <u>safeharborministry@comcast.net</u> or write
    Safe Harbor Ministry
    P.O. Box 456
    Toms River NJ 08754